Will You Go With Me?

by Wiley Blevins

Ken Cavanagh/McGraw-Hill Education

I can read.

A B C.

Ken Cavanagh/McGraw-Hill Education

I am ready for Kindergarten.

Antonova Anna/Shutterstock.com

I can count.

1 2 3 4 5 6 7 8 9 10.

I am ready for Kindergarten.

wavebreakmedia/Shutterstock.com

I can write.

I am ready for Kindergarten.

Ken Cavanagh/McGraw-Hill Education

Will you go with me?